BLUE BANNER
BIOGRAPHY

SELENA

Joanne Mattern

Mitchell Lane

PUBLISHERS

P.O. Box 196
Hockessin, Delaware 19707
Visit us on the web: www.mitchelllane.com
Comments? email us: mitchelllane@mitchelllane.com

Mitchell Lane

PUBLISHERS

Printing   1   2   3   4   5   6   7   8   9

Blue Banner Biographies

Alicia Keys	Gwen Stefani	Megan Fox
Allen Iverson	Ice Cube	Miguel Tejada
Ashanti	Ja Rule	Nancy Pelosi
Ashlee Simpson	Jamie Foxx	Natasha Bedingfield
Ashton Kutcher	Jay-Z	Orianthi
Avril Lavigne	Jennifer Lopez	Orlando Bloom
Beyoncé	Jessica Simpson	P. Diddy
Blake Lively	J. K. Rowling	Peyton Manning
Bow Wow	Joe Flacco	Pink
Brett Favre	John Legend	Prince William
Britney Spears	Justin Berfield	Queen Latifah
CC Sabathia	Justin Timberlake	Rihanna
Carrie Underwood	Kanye West	Robert Downey Jr.
Chris Brown	Kate Hudson	Robert Pattinson
Chris Daughtry	Katy Perry	Ron Howard
Christina Aguilera	Keith Urban	Sean Kingston
Ciara	Kelly Clarkson	Selena
Clay Aiken	Kenny Chesney	Shakira
Cole Hamels	Ke$ha	Shia LaBeouf
Condoleezza Rice	Kristen Stewart	Shontelle Layne
Corbin Bleu	Lady Gaga	Soulja Boy Tell 'Em
Daniel Radcliffe	Lance Armstrong	Stephenie Meyer
David Ortiz	Leona Lewis	Taylor Swift
David Wright	Lil Wayne	T.I.
Derek Jeter	Lindsay Lohan	Timbaland
Drew Brees	Ludacris	Tim McGraw
Eminem	Mariah Carey	Toby Keith
Eve	Mario	Usher
Fergie	Mary J. Blige	Vanessa Anne Hudgens
Flo Rida	Mary-Kate and Ashley Olsen	Zac Efron

Library of Congress Cataloging-in-Publication Data
Mattern, Joanne, 1963–
 Selena / by Joanne Mattern.
    p. cm. — (Blue banner biographies)
 Includes bibliographical references and index.
 ISBN 978-1-61228-054-7 (library bound)
 1. Selena, 1971–1995—Juvenile literature. 2. Tejano musicians—Biography—Juvenile literature. I. Title.
 ML3930.S43M38 2012
 782.42164092—dc22
 [B]
                                                                                    2011016782
eBook ISBN: 9781612281810

ABOUT THE AUTHOR: Joanne Mattern has written more than 250 children's books, including *Blake Lively, Ashley Tisdale, Peyton Manning, The Jonas Brothers,* and *LeBron James* for Mitchell Lane Publishers. She lives in New York State with her husband, four children, and several pets.

PUBLISHER'S NOTE: The following story has been thoroughly researched, and to the best of our knowledge represents a true story. While every possible effort has been made to ensure accuracy, the publisher will not assume liability for damages caused by inaccuracies in the data and makes no warranty on the accuracy of the information contained herein. This story has not been authorized or endorsed by Selena Quintanilla-Peréz or her family.

BLUE BANNER BIOGRAPHY

Selena wows the crowd at a concert in 1995, when she was at the peak of her fame. Just one month later, tragedy would end her life.

Selena ¡Vive!

*O*n April 7, 2005, fans of Hispanic music gathered at Reliant Stadium in Houston, Texas. They were there to celebrate the life and music of one of Tejano music's most beloved stars: Selena.

Latina musician and actress Jennifer Lopez opened the show. She was followed by many of Latin music's biggest stars. For three hours, more than 50,000 fans danced and sang along to singers and bands. Some of the featured guests were Thalía, Banda el Recodo, Ana Barbara, Pablo Montero, and Ana Gabriel.

Selena's family also took part in the show. Her brother, A.B. Quintanilla, provided one of the most touching moments of the concert, performing a special duet with his sister. He sang with a recording of Selena on her hit "Baila Esta Cumbia." His band, the Kumbia Kings, accompanied him.

Along with musical performances, the concert also included videos of Selena performing. Other videos told the story of her backup band, Los Dinos, and Selena's impact as a role model for young women. Then the crowd was treated to more music, performed by such popular Latin artists as Montéz de Durango, Graciela Beltrán, Bobby Pulido, Jay Pérez, and Alejandra Guzmán. These musicians performed their own versions of Selena's biggest hits.

The show ended with an emotional performance for the entire crowd. As a video of Selena performing her song "Como La Flor" played on a giant video screen, Los Dinos played the song live on stage. The crowd sang along and waved white roses. Then all of the evening's performers returned to the stage, accompanied by a 55-member children's chorus. Together, everyone sang the song as a tribute to the Tejano queen.

"The evening exceeded our wildest expectations. Selena's memory is very much alive . . ."

The Selena ¡Vive! Reunion Concert was a phenomenon all over the Latin world. Besides the 50,000 people in the stadium, the network Univision broadcast the concert to countries with Spanish audiences. Millions of people all over the world watched this television special.

Selena's family was overwhelmed by the success of the concert. Afterward, her father, Abraham Quintanilla, told reporters, "The evening exceeded our wildest expectations. Selena's memory is very much alive as witnessed by the outpouring of emotions during tonight's event."

There was only one person missing from the amazing evening: Selena. Although she appeared in old videos and performances, Selena could not attend the concert in her

These fans are some of the 50,000 people who packed Reliant Stadium for the Selena ¡Vive! Reunion Concert in 2005. Even ten years after her death, Selena remained hugely popular.

honor. She had been murdered ten years earlier, at the age of twenty-three. The tragedy of her death rocked the Latin world. However, it also introduced Selena to millions of fans who had not known anything about her or the Tejano music scene.

Selena's story continues to fascinate and inspire music fans. Her music is still extremely popular, and she has fans all over the world. Some of these fans were not even born when Selena died in 1995.

Selena's parents, Marcella and Abraham Quintanilla, were strict but loving heads of the family. "We grew up with morals and also respect for everyone," Selena once said of her parents. "My father always treated us equal."

CHAPTER 2

Family Ties

Music was an important part of Selena's family life even before she was born. Her father, Abraham Quintanilla Jr., had played in bands since he was in high school. During the late 1950s and early 1960s, Abraham was part of a band called The Dinos ("The Boys"). The Dinos played at parties in and around their hometown of Corpus Christi, Texas.

In 1961, Abraham was drafted into the army. While he was stationed in Washington State, he met Marcella Samora. Abraham and Marcella fell in love and got married. Soon the family grew to include their first child, a son named Abraham III. The little boy was always called A.B.

After he finished his army service, Abraham moved his family back to south Texas. Once again, he became active in the local music scene. At that time, a type of music called Tejano was becoming very popular among the Hispanic population in Texas. Tejano music combines elements of American rock and country music with traditional Mexican and Spanish sounds from accordions, keyboards, and twelve-string guitars. The music is lively and fast, and the songs are sung in Spanish.

Abraham rejoined his high school band and changed its name slightly to Los Dinos. The band began performing the new Tejano style. In 1967, Abraham and Marcella welcomed their second child, a girl named Suzette. Abraham was on the road with Los Dinos and couldn't make it home in time for the birth. He missed his family and knew he had to spend more time with them.

> *"I was a little tomboy when I was growing up. I used to like to play football with the guys . . ."*

In 1969, Abraham quit Los Dinos. He got a job at a chemical plant and moved his family to Lake Jackson, Texas. There, on April 16, 1971, the family welcomed a third child, a girl named Selena.

Selena had a normal childhood. She enjoyed many childhood games with her brother and sister and the other children in the neighborhood. She later wrote on her web site, "I was a little tomboy when I was growing up. I used to like to play football with the guys and you know, normal things like hide-and-seek, and get a hold of my brother's bike and try to teach myself how to ride it."

Although Selena's life was like other children's in many ways, there were some big differences. Selena and her family were members of a strict religion called Jehovah's Witnesses. As part of their faith, they did not celebrate birthdays or most other holidays. In addition, music was still a huge part of the Quintanillas' everyday life. Abraham taught A.B. how to play guitar. He also taught Suzette how to play the drums. Five-year-old

Selena clowns around with her sister, Suzette. The two were extremely close and spent most of their time together, both on and off the stage.

Selena wanted to join in the fun. Instead of learning an instrument, she opened her mouth and sang.

Everyone was surprised at how big and pure Selena's voice was. She had a natural talent and rhythm. Selena's father was pleased. "Her timing and her pitch were perfect," he told *People* magazine in 1995. "I could see it from day one."

Selena's talent gave Abraham a chance to fulfill a dream. "I always wanted to go back into the music business, but I felt like I was already getting too old," he said in an interview with Rick Mitchell of the *Houston Chronicle*. "When I found out Selena could sing, that's when the wheels started turning

Selena poses with her band, Los Dinos. Los Dinos was like a second family to Selena and included members of her real family as well.

in my mind. I saw a chance to get back in the music world through my kids."

The Quintanillas began to perform at family gatherings and local events. At first, Selena sang in English. However, her father realized that she had to learn Spanish if she was to sing the Tejano songs that were so popular in southern Texas. He began to teach her to sing in Spanish by sounding out the words. By the time she grew up, she could sing and speak Spanish very well.

At first, Selena and her siblings weren't sure they liked Tejano music. Like most children, they preferred the pop music they heard on the radio. Selena recalled that when her father first introduced the children to Tejano music, they said, "'No, you can't make us play it.' There were times we would come in to practice and we would start crying, 'We don't want to learn this music.' But we learned it and now that's all we listen to on the radio and we like to play it." On her web site, Selena described Tejano music as "a fusion of a lot of different types of music all rolled into one package. It's country music, it's jazz, it has roots of German polka, it also has Mexican music in it. Tejano music is a very relaxing style and it reminds me of home."

> "It's country music, it's jazz, it has roots of German polka, it also has Mexican music in it. Tejano music is a very relaxing style . . ."

In 1980, Abraham and a friend opened a Mexican restaurant called Papagayo's. Along with good food, the restaurant also featured good music. Southern Pearl, a local country-western band, often performed at the restaurant, and Selena would sing lead vocals. She was only nine years old, but she loved to be onstage. She sang and danced and performed like someone much older.

She even recorded a song with Southern Pearl for a local disc jockey. They were thrilled when the song was played on the radio. "She's going places," the disc jockey told Selena's father. "She's got it all—the voice, moves, the smile." However, it would be a few more years before Selena and her family hit the big time.

Selena loved to let loose onstage and often wore flashy costumes as she danced. But off stage, she confessed, "I don't dance with strangers unless they ask my dad for permission."

CHAPTER 3

Teen Queen of Tejano

When the oil business went bust in Texas, Papagayo's had to close. Money was so scarce, the family lost their home. Abraham and his family decided to focus on Tejano music, and they started touring southern Texas in their van. Selena continued to learn songs in Spanish, and Abraham passed on the name of his old band to the family band. He hoped people would remember the original Los Dinos. He also knew a Spanish name would attract more attention than an English name in the Tejano world.

Selena attended school, but spent most of her free time practicing and performing. The band started out at bars and weddings and moved up to ballrooms. Meanwhile they released several albums on a regional record label. The schedule was difficult. Los Dinos often traveled out of town on weekends, and Selena often missed school on Fridays and Mondays. Her teachers complained about how much time she missed, but the young girl always made up her work. She got good grades and performed well in school spelling bees and other events.

By the mid 1980s, the band was known as Selena y Los Dinos, and they were touring in a bus they dubbed Big Bertha. They were becoming better known in Texas. Their song "Oh, Mama" was played on the radio. This success led to an appearance on a local television show called *The Johnny Canales Show*. This program was one of the most popular Spanish television shows in south Texas and Mexico.

It was getting harder and harder for Selena to attend school. Also, her father believed that performing would be

Selena began recording when she was very young. By the time she was a teenager, she was very comfortable in a recording studio.

Selena's career, not academics. In eighth grade, he pulled her out of school, but education remained very important to her. She studied through a correspondence course, and in 1989, she received her GED (general equivalency diploma). She took several business courses as well.

Abraham kept a tight rein on his family. He booked all their performances and made sure they were paid fairly and on time. No one, including his children, argued with him. He expected Selena, Suzette, and A.B. to act like professionals, no matter what. If they were sick or tired or just in a bad mood, they still had to perform and do a great job.

Selena adored her parents and her siblings. She later wrote on her web site, "What's good about our family is that we've all had the same goal and we all have the same respect for my father. We don't hold grudges and I think that's sort of been the key to the success. We have our disagreements but whether we're right or wrong, we'll just go and apologize." Selena also described her mother as "loving, sentimental, honest, uncomplicated. My mom is everything that is good."

When Selena was fifteen, a magazine called *Tejano Entertainer* featured a photo of her on the cover. The magazine called her the youngest female singer on the Tejano circuit. The article drew more attention to the band. Radio stations began to play more of the band's music. Soon Selena y Los Dinos had several number-one hits on Texas radio stations.

In 1987, the band was nominated for a number of awards at the Tejano Music Awards. Selena was excited to be nominated for Female Vocalist of the Year. She was even more thrilled and surprised when she won! She and the band won several other awards that year. The band took notice of their success in the title of the album they released in 1987: *And the Winner Is . . .*

Selena went on to win Female Vocalist of the Year at the Tejano Music Awards several more times. By 1989, she was famous in the Latino communities of Texas and Mexico. That same year, she signed a contract with a major record company called Capitol-EMI Latin Records. Capitol planned to promote her to Latin markets outside of Texas.

Selena got more recognition when she became a spokesperson for Coca-Cola. This deal earned her and her family a lot of money. It also made her more well-known and popular in the wider Latin community. The executives at Coca-Cola were impressed at Selena's poise and professionalism. In Joe Patoski's biography of Selena, one executive, Lionel Sosa, recalled how great it was to work with her. "She was just wonderful to everybody, whether it was the assistant at a shoot or the president of Coca-Cola. She knew who everybody was, went out and hugged them, and made it seem like it was a privilege for her to be doing what she was doing. You always got that feeling, like she thought, 'I'm so lucky to be here.' "

> *By 1990, Selena had grown into a beautiful and confident young woman. . . . She was a solo star.*

By 1990, Selena had grown into a beautiful and confident young woman. That year, she won both Female Entertainer of the Year and Female Vocalist of the Year at the Tejano Music Awards. Her new album, *Ven Conmigo (Come With Me)*, marked a change in the band. For the first time, only Selena was listed on the cover. Los Dinos was now her backup band. Selena was a solo star.

CHAPTER 4

Love and Success

By the early 1990s, Selena was recognized as the Queen of Tejano. She and her family and band members toured all over Mexico and the southwestern United States. Their albums sold well, and fans packed their shows wherever they performed.

One fan was especially persistent. Yolanda Saldívar was devoted to Selena. She called herself "the biggest Selena fan." Saldívar approached Abraham and Suzette and asked to start a fan club. After thinking about it for a while, Abraham agreed. Saldívar was put in charge of the club. She mailed newsletters, posters, and merchandise to fans and kept track of the dues each fan paid. She was also supposed to donate some of the money to charity. In time, Saldívar and Selena became close friends.

Meanwhile, Selena was becoming close to someone else outside her family. Over the years, Abraham had hired additional musicians to join Los Dinos to give the band a fuller sound. One of these musicians was guitarist Chris Peréz. His unique style combined traditional Tejano sounds

Selena accepts her Grammy for the Selena Live *album. When her name was announced, "We got up and we screamed," Selena recalled. "I cried in the back. It was just a great feeling."*

with hard-rock guitar. He and Selena became friends, and over time, they fell in love.

Selena and Peréz wanted to get married, but she knew her father would never allow her to marry the young musician. Finally, she could not stand to be apart from the love of her life. On April 2, 1992, she and Peréz slipped away and got married. Selena later recalled on her web site that she had always dreamed of a big wedding, but she chose to elope and have a simple ceremony. "My love for Chris was so strong, I couldn't wait any longer for us to be husband and wife."

Abraham was very angry when he found out what Selena had done. It was the first time she had defied him. However, he soon realized that Selena and Peréz did love each other, and Selena was a grown woman who could make her own decisions. The couple moved into their own house near the rest of the family.

The next two years brought Selena more happiness and success than she had ever dreamed of. Her albums *Entre a Mi Mundo (Welcome to My World)* and *Amor Prohibido (Forbidden Love)* were huge successes. She was honored in 1994 when she won a Grammy for *Selena Live* as Best Mexican-American Album. This live album captured the joy of Selena's performances. She once said, "When I'm singing I'm a completely different person. I could be very free. What I do on stage, you won't catch me doing off stage. I think deep down I'm still kind of timid and modest about a lot of things. But on stage, I release all that; I let it go."

Selena also filmed commercials for a variety of products, including shampoo and a local telephone company. She even appeared in a Mexican soap opera and had a tiny part in the movie *Don Juan DeMarco*, starring Johnny Depp.

> "My love for Chris was so strong, I couldn't wait any longer for us to be husband and wife."

Along with music, Selena had always loved fashion. Over the years, she had designed many of her stage costumes. By 1994, she had started her own fashion line called Selena, Etc. She also opened several beauty salons and boutiques in Texas. She hired Saldívar to help her manage all these ventures.

Although she spent most of her time on the road, Selena was quick to help people in need. She visited schools and talked to students about the importance of education. She also encouraged students to stay away from drugs and to make the most of their lives. She performed at a benefit concert after Hurricane Andrew devastated part of south Florida in 1992.

The year 1995 was the most successful of Selena's career. Her latest album, *Dreaming of You*, was nearly ready to be released. It featured songs in English and Spanish and would introduce Selena to an audience beyond the Hispanic market. In February, she performed to a sold-out crowd at the Astrodome in Houston. *Hispanic Business* magazine named Selena "one of the most successful Latin entertainers in the world." It seemed as if nothing could stop Selena's joy.

> **Although she spent most of her time on the road, Selena was quick to help people in need.**

CHAPTER 5

Selena Lives On

*E*arly in 1995, Abraham began receiving complaints from members of Selena's fan club. They said they had sent in their dues but had not received their merchandise. Money was also missing from Selena's boutique in Corpus Christi. Abraham went over the business's bank accounts and discovered that Yolanda Saldívar had written checks to herself totaling more than $3,000. He angrily confronted her. He demanded that she explain what had happened and return the missing money.

On March 31, 1995, Saldívar arranged to meet Selena alone at a motel in Corpus Christi. The two women argued, and Selena fired Saldívar from her position as president of the fan club. Saldívar became very upset. She pulled out a gun and shot Selena in the back. Selena was rushed to a hospital, but she died of blood loss just after one o'clock that afternoon.

Selena's death was a huge shock to her family and fans. "She was starting to bloom, not only as a person but as an artist," her father said during an emotional news conference. "She was a very loving person. She cared for people."

Candlelight vigils were held all across Texas, and people sent thousands of flowers and cards to the Quintanilla home.

Almost 60,000 people lined up to view Selena's body at a wake held at a convention center in Corpus Christi. Tens of thousands also attended her funeral, and fans gathered for services in other cities as well.

Saldívar was arrested and eventually sentenced to life in prison. She claimed that the shooting was an accident.

In the years after Selena's death, her fans and family did not forget the Tejano queen. Each year, thousands of people visit her grave.

Although she ended Selena's life, she did not end the singer's fame and influence. As one fan told reporter Richard Jerome after the trial, "Saldívar thinks she killed Selena, but she only made her more alive, because more people know of her now."

In the years after Selena's death, her fans and family did not forget the Tejano queen. Each year, thousands of people visit her grave. Corpus Christi built a memorial to her. The monument, called Mirador de la Flor (Overlook of the Flower), faces the sea.

So many people visited the family's business offices that the Quintanillas opened a Selena museum there. The museum has many items that belonged to Selena, including several of her stage costumes and dresses.

The Quintanillas also decided to honor Selena by helping others. They used the donations they received from fans to start the Selena Foundation. This charity's mission is "to offer the motivation that every child needs to continue

Every year, fans gather outside Selena's home in Corpus Christi on the anniversary of her death. Even very young fans who were not born when Selena was performing come to honor the fallen star.

Many fans protested Jennifer Lopez's casting as Selena in the movie because Lopez is Puerto Rican, not Mexican. Lopez also found the role difficult because, she said, "Selena isn't a fictional character — and her family is sitting right in front of me while I'm acting." Despite these issues, the movie went on to become a huge hit and made Lopez a star.

their education, to live moral lives, to love their families, to respect human life, and to sing whatever song they were born to sing."

A.B. completed *Dreaming of You* and released it in July 1995. The album was a huge success, entering the Billboard 200 album chart at number one. It was the first time a Latino artist had achieved this feat.

Abraham Quintanilla wanted more people to know his daughter's story. In 1997, the movie *Selena* was released. This story of the singer's life starred Jennifer Lopez. At that time, Lopez was known as a singer and actress, and the movie made her even more famous. *Selena* was a hit, earning more than $35 million in the United States alone. "I think the movie exposed [Selena] to a lot of different people," A.B. told reporter Leila Cobo.

Selena's family has continued to make music. A.B. created and played in the popular Tejano band Kumbia Kings. Later, as band members changed, his band was called A.B. Quintanilla's All-Starz. Chris Peréz plays guitar for several groups, including the All-Starz.

Selena remains one of the best-loved and popular Latina stars, and since her death, Latin music has become even more popular.

Selena remains one of the best-loved and popular Latina stars, and since her death, Latin music has become even more popular all across the United States. Her music and influence will not soon be forgotten.

1971   Selena Quintanilla is born on April 16 in Lake Jackson, Texas.

1976   Selena begins singing with her family.

1980   Selena and her siblings perform regularly at her family's restaurant, Papagayo's.

1983   The Quintanillas move to Corpus Christi; the family tours as Selena y Los Dinos.

1984   Selena leaves school to tour full-time.

1986   She is featured on the cover of *Tejano Entertainer*.

1987   She wins her first Female Vocalist of the Year Award at the Tejano Music Awards.

1989   Selena signs with Capitol-EMI Latin Records; she becomes a spokesperson for Coca-Cola. She earns her GED.

1990   Selena wins Female Entertainer of the Year and Female Vocalist of the Year at the Tejano Music Awards.

1992   Selena marries guitarist Chris Peréz on April 2. After Hurricane Andrew, she performs in a benefit concert to rebuild south Florida.

1993   Her father, Abraham, founds Q Productions, a company that produces Latino musicians.

1994   Selena wins a Grammy Award for Best Mexican-American album for *Selena Live*; she introduces her Selena, Etc. fashion line, and opens a beauty salon and boutique in Corpus Christi. Yolanda Saldívar helps manage these businesses.

1995   Saldívar kills Selena on March 31; Selena's album *Dreaming of You* debuts at number one on the Billboard 200 album chart; the Quintanilla family starts the Selena Foundation; Saldívar is sentenced to life in prison for Selena's murder.

1997   The movie *Selena*, starring Jennifer Lopez, is released; a memorial statue of Selena is dedicated in Corpus Christi.

1998   The Selena Museum opens in Corpus Christi.

2005   Latin music stars perform at the Selena ¡Vive! Reunion Concert to honor Selena on the tenth anniversary of her death.

2011 On March 16, the U.S. Postal Service releases a stamp to commemorate Selena as part of its Latin Music Legends collection. Digital sales of her music increase, with six of her songs in the top twenty musical downloads on Billboard's Regional Mexican Digital Songs chart.

DISCOGRAPHY

1995	*Dreaming of You*	**1988**	*Dulce Amor*
1994	*Amor Prohibido*	**1987**	*And the Winner Is . . .*
1993	*Selena Live*	**1986**	*Alpha*
1992	*Entre a Mi Mundo*		*Muñequito de Trapo*
1990	*Ven Conmigo*	**1985**	*The New Girl In Town*
1989	*Selena*	**1984**	*Mis Primeras Grabaciones*
1988	*Preciosa*		

Works Consulted

Alford, Steven. "Selena Fans Gather for Annual Tribute on Anniversary of Singer's Death." *Corpus Christi Caller-Times*, April 1, 2011. http://www.caller.com/news/2011/apr/01/selena-fans-gather-for-annual-tribute-on-of/?partner=yahoo_feeds

Arraras, Maria Celeste. *Selena's Secret: The Revealing Story Behind Her Tragic Death.* New York: Simon & Schuster, 1997.

Cobo, Leila. "Selena." *Hispanic Magazine*, April 2005, Vol. 10, Issue 3.

———. "Selena—The Legend, 10 Years Later." *Hispanic Magazine*, June 2005. http://www.banderasnews.com/0506/ent-selena.htm

———. "U.S. Stamp Sparks Selena Digital Track Sales." *Billboard.biz*, April 1, 2011. http://www.billboard.biz/bbbiz/others/en-breve-u-s-stamp-sparks-selena-digital-1005107882.story

Gianoulis, Tina. "Selena." *St. James Encyclopedia of Popular Culture*, January 29, 2002. http://findarticles.com/p/articles/mi_g1epc/is_bio/ai_2419201088/

Hewitt, Bill. "Before Her Time." *People*, April 17, 1995. http://www.people.com/people/archive/article/0,,20105524,00.html

Jerome, Richard. "Resolution." *People*, November 6, 1995. http://www.people.com/people/archive/article/0,,20147270,00.html

Lambert, Pam. "¡Vive Selena!" *People*, March 24, 1997. http://www.people.com/people/archive/article/0,,20143782,00.html

Menard, Valerie. "The Making of Selena." *Hispanic Magazine*, March 1997, Vol. 10, Issue 3.

Mitchell, Rick. "In Life, She Was the Queen of Tejano Music. In Death, the 23-year-old Singer Is Becoming a Legend." *Houston Chronicle*, 1995. http://selenatrial.selenaforever.com/

Patoski, Joe Nick. *Selena: Como la Flor.* Boston: Little Brown and Co., 1996; excerpted by the *Houston Chronicle* at http://selenatrial.selenaforever.com/Selena_Archive/3_31_96a.html.

"Selena." *People* Magazine Special Tribute Issue, April 24, 1995.

Selena. Q-Productions, Inc. Warner Home Video, 1997.

Strauss, Chris. "Still Dreaming of Selena." *People*, April 4, 2005. http://www.people.com/people/archive/article/0,,20147270,00.html

Univision Press Release: "Univision's Selena ¡Vive! Breaks Audience Records." April 11, 2005. http://www.univision.net/corp/en/pr/Houston_11042005-2.html

Zapata, John. "Selena, Mi Amiga." Tejano Entertainment Network, n.d., http://tejanoentertainment.net/artists/selena

Books

Drake-Boyt, Elizabeth. *Latin Dance.* Westport, CT: Greenwood Publishing, 2011.

Lemmens, MaryJo. *Jennifer Lopez.* Broomall, PA: Mason Crest Publishers, 2008.

Lindeen, Mary. *Cool Latin Music: Create & Appreciate What Makes Music Great!* Edina, MN: Abdo, 2008.

Tsoukanelis, Erika Alexia. *The Latin Music Scene: The Stars, the Fans, the Music.* Berkeley Heights, NJ: Enslow Publishers, Inc., 2009.

Wong, Adam. *Jennifer Lopez.* New York: Chelsea House, 2008.

On the Internet

A.B. Quintanilla's All-Starz
http://www.abquintanilla3.com/

Q-Productions
http://www.q-productions.com

Selena (1997, movie)
http://www.imdb.com/title/tt0120094/

Selena Forever
http://www.selenaforever.com

The Selena Foundation
http://www.q-productions.com/selenafoundation.html

Tejano Reina
http://www.tejanoreina.com

INDEX